Writers and th(
A critical and biblio(

Ge ral E(
Ian cott-Kuvert

Mark Gerson

TOM STOPPARD

TOM STOPPARD

by
C. W. E. BIGSBY

PUBLISHED FOR
THE BRITISH COUNCIL
BY LONGMAN GROUP LTD

LONGMAN GROUP LTD
Longman House, Burnt Mill, Harlow, Essex

*Associated companies, branches and
representatives throughout the world*

First published 1976
Revised 1979
© C. W. E. Bigsby 1976

*Printed in England by
Eyre and Spottiswoode Limited
at Grosvenor Press Portsmouth*

ISBN 0 582 01251 1

TOM STOPPARD

'Don't you see that nowadays tragedy isn't possible any more?
... Today farce is the only thing possible.'
(*Tango*, by Sławomir Mrożek, translated by Tom Stoppard)

In the early 1960s the English theatre seemed suddenly to have found itself. It celebrated with naïve enthusiasm its belated discovery of naturalism and its new-found social concern. For a brief period playwrights tended to regard themselves as the cutting edge of a social revolution in which they would articulate the frustration of a new generation growing up in a society that seemed not merely complacent to the point of inertia but dangerously blind to the vital forces which lay encysted within a decaying art. Despite the fact that this fervour gave birth to a disturbing sentimentality rather than hard-edged social or political analysis, the energy which had been released so suddenly created a compelling paradigm for the new writer. As Tom Stoppard has said, 'after 1956 everybody my age who wanted to write, wanted to write plays—after Osborne and the rest at the Court'.

But if increased financial support for the arts, the creation of major subsidized companies, the expansion of television services and the growth of regional drama encouraged many young writers to work for the stage, it did not create an *avant-garde* studiously dedicated to fracturing the mould of twentieth-century drama. The newly liberated imagination largely turned to familiar forms; the revolution, it seemed, had more to do with renewal than iconoclasm. Certainly, despite the much publicized working-class and Jewish origins of some new writers, the public school, Oxford and Cambridge, continued to provide us with the majority of our dramatists. What these new writers did offer, however, was a control of language that placed them in a recognizable English tradition which in the previous half century had produced Wilde, Shaw and Coward. Pre-eminent among these is Tom Stoppard who combines considerable talents as a parodist and wit with a genuinely personal vision. Recognizably derivative in his early work, he has emerged as a writer of genuine originality.

Stoppard was born in 1937 in Zlin, Czechoslovakia. His father worked for the internationally famous Bata shoe company, and when the Germans threatened invasion the family was transferred to the Singapore branch. Three years later they were forced to move again when Japanese troops captured the city. Stoppard's father was killed; with his mother and brother he was evacuated to India. Here his mother remarried and the family name became Stoppard.

On their return to England in 1946, he attended a preparatory school in Nottinghamshire and a boarding grammar school in Yorkshire, and in 1954 he began his career as a journalist, working first for the *Western Daily Press* and subsequently for the *Bristol Evening World*. As a theatre reviewer he became interested in writing for the stage: in 1960 he resigned his job and in three months wrote *A Walk on the Water*. This was eventually bought by a commercial television company, and Stoppard's public career as a playwright began in November 1963. After several rewrites and a brief production in Hamburg, the play was finally produced on the London stage, two years after the success of *Rosencrantz and Guildenstern are Dead*, under a new title, *Enter a Free Man*.

Stoppard is a self-confessed aesthetic reactionary. That is, at a time when the *avant-garde* in theatre is de-emphasizing language, stressing performance over text, preferring group composition to the insights of the individual author, he believes in the primacy of words. At a time when committed artists are asserting that art necessarily derives from social commitment, he regards it at times as a formalist exercise and at others as a moral gesture. As he has explained, 'I don't set out ... to write a play that will demand a new kind of theatre or a new kind of audience. But my feeling still is that the theatre ought to start from writing, come what may, even though in my view it is a delusion that a play is the end product of an idea; in my experience the idea is the end product of the play.' In an article entitled 'Something to Declare', published in 1968, he confessed that he had 'very few social preoccupations', writing, instead, out of a love of language and an avowedly intellectual fascination with 'things I find difficult to express'. 'Some writers', he continued, 'write because they burn with a cause which they further by writing about it. I burn with no causes. I cannot say that I write with any social objective. One writes because one loves writing.'[1] When he adds that he is 'hooked on style', however, he is not only describing his own concern as a writer, but is also identifying the desperate strategy of so many of his protagonists who feel, in the words of a character from his only novel, *Lord Malquist and Mr Moon*, that

> since we cannot hope for order let us withdraw with style from chaos.

Lord Malquist and Mr Moon (1966) is an exuberant farce, an absurdist romp which displays his considerable talent for parody, the opening chapter offering a collage of literary styles used to ironic effect. His methodology is reminiscent of Salvador Dali in so far as he treats improbable situations in a realistic manner, bringing together radically dissimilar elements. He peoples his novel with a black Irish Jew, two cowboys who stage a shoot-out in Trafalgar Square, a man who regards himself as the Risen Christ, and a peer of the realm who insists on behaving as though he were living in the eighteenth century, while assiduously seducing the wife of his biographer, an historian turned anarchist. This latter has set himself the somewhat daunting task of writing a history of the world, in the conviction that with perseverance it will manifest a coherent order which he not unnaturally finds hard to distinguish in the chaotic events which buffet him daily. The first and only sentence which he has thus far composed for his great work has unfortunately so unnerved him, however, that he is unable to get any further. Having written the confident words, 'History is the progress of Man in the World, and the beginning of history is the beginning of Man' he can write only the word 'Therefore', before the demonstrable absurdity of his premise overwhelms him. Half recognizing the fallacy implicit in his own capital letters, he wanders through London equipped with a home-made bomb, none too sure whether he wishes to precipitate the chaos which he feels to be implicit

[1] *Sunday Times*, 25 February 1968.

in human affairs, or to rectify some mistake which has inadvertently caused an otherwise reliable system to malfunction. He finds himself 'without possibility of reprieve or hope of explanation', bemused by the bewildering anarchy of existence, and uncertain whether life would be more absurd if it were random or simply the mechanical enactment of a determined scenario. It is thus entirely consistent that the novel should be full of characters more distinguished for their bizarre life-styles than for their authentic humanity for they, like Moon, appear to have grasped a truth which Stoppard himself adheres to with apparent conviction, until *Jumpers* and *Travesties* reveals a tentative humanism which had in fact always lurked beneath his absurdist stance; they have understood, that is, that 'substance is ephemeral but style is eternal', an assumption which though it 'may not be a solution to the realities of life . . . is a workable alternative'. Stoppard seems to suggest with Wilde that life may best be regarded as an imitation of art, that in a situation where nothing can be taken seriously farce is both the true realism and, by a kind of homeopathic logic, the only valid strategy for artist and individual alike. Yet this conviction seems to battle with a more deep-seated humanism which leads him not only to reveal a compassionate concern for his characters but also to advocacy of such a concern within otherwise absurdist dramas. For, after all, as one of his characters observes in *Jumpers*, 'the whole point of denying the Absolute was to reduce the scale, instantly, to the inconsequential behaviour of inconsequential animals.' Yet this logic is too implacable for Stoppard. He creates a series of characters who, although ultimately defeated by social and metaphysical forces, provoke or themselves embrace a human compassion which transcends the relativistic ethics of an absurd universe.

In his early plays he presents a series of images of the individual trapped inside a mechanistic world, warped and destroyed by a logical system which fails to accommodate itself to human aspirations. *If You're Glad I'll be Frank* (1969) details the ineffectual rebellion of the telephonist who works as the speaking clock. In the battle between her fragile individualism and the social and mechanical forces there can be only one victor. Like her lover, whose protests have to be accommodated to the schedules of his regular bus route, the most she can do is stutter out her protest before retreating once more into her social role. In *Albert's Bridge* (1969) the same battle is repeated, except that Albert actually embraces his mechanical job as a release from the alarming disorder of his mundane existence. Albert takes great pleasure in his career as painter on the Clufton Bay Bridge, discovering poetry in its symmetry and meaning in its geometrical precision. His own life lacks this coherence, human relations stubbornly refusing to display the patterned grace and predictable order of the machine. He abandons his wife and withdraws into the reassuring world of the bridge, attracted by the fact that it is 'separate—complete—removed, defined by principles of engineering which makes it stop at a certain point, which compels a certain shape, certain joints—the whole thing utterly fixed by the rules that make it stay up ... complete'. But the same logical rules which enabled the bridge to be built also lead to its collapse when an army of painters march across it without breaking step. In other words the existence of order and system do not of themselves imply purpose and meaning. Albert discovers order in narcissism only to perish like Narcissus.

The note in these early plays is one of compassionate irony. Faced with a situation which seems to offer '*nothing*, absolutely nothing', in which 'I give nothing, I gain nothing, it is nothing', George Riley's conviction that 'A man must resist. A man must stand apart, make a clear break on his own two feet,' that 'faith is the key—faith in oneself' becomes merely ironic. It is a faith which can only be sustained so long as he refuses to recognize his absolute dependence on those around him, on the absurd fictions which he chooses to embrace. Like Willy Loman[1] he seems to feel that the stars projected on the clouds from the rooftops are real stars. As with Willy Loman the consequence is a combination of pathos and a curious dignity. In such a world the only value is indeed compassion.

Stoppard has confessed that *A Walk on the Water* was in fact *Flowering Death of a Salesman*,[2] admitting that 'I don't

---

[1] The leading character in Arthur Miller's *Death of a Salesman*.
[2] A combination of Robert Bolt's *Flowering Cherry* with *Death of a Salesman*.

think it's a very true play, in the sense that I feel no intimacy with the people I was writing about. It works pretty well as a play, but it's actually phony because it's a play written about other people's characters.'[1] Certainly *Enter a Free Man*, the re-written stage version which was eventually produced in 1968 following the success of *Rosencrantz and Guildenstern are Dead*, is a curiously eclectic work. Indeed, a number of speeches could have come straight out of Miller, as, for example, when the play's protagonist, George Riley, laments that,

'My life is piled up between me and the sun, as real and hopeless as a pile of broken furniture. Thirty years ago I was a young man ready to leave the ground and fly. Thirty years . . . More, perhaps much more than the time I have left, and when a man's past outweighs his future, then he's a man standing in his own shadow.'

There is the same tension between father and child as in *Death of a Salesman*, the same desperate attachment to illusion sustained by a wife every bit as compassionate and understanding as Linda in Miller's play. Stoppard even retains the name Linda, transferring it to the daughter.

Yet, despite this, Stoppard's own voice is clear enough, and in the figure of George Riley he creates the first of many portraits of a modern hero. Riley is a man who has dedicated his life to perfecting such devices as a re-usable envelope (with gum on both sides of the flap) and an elaborate system of pipes designed to utilize rainfall to water indoor plants. Unaware of the logical flaws which make his inventions useless, he nonetheless pits his 'tattered dignity' against a world which seems designed merely to taunt him. Described in the stage directions as 'a smallish untidy figure in a crumpled suit . . . certainly not mad but . . . definitely odd', he is, we are assured, 'unsinkable, despite the slow leak'. And this 'tattered dignity' is what characterizes the Stoppard hero, for while it is clear that none of his characters control their own destiny, that neither logic nor faith can confer meaning on their lives, it is equally obvious that their unsinkable quality, their irrepressible vitality and eccentric persistence, constitute what Stoppard feels to be an authentic response to existence. They are marginal men, uncertain of their own role and unsure of

---

[1] 'Ambushes for the Audience', *Theatre Quarterly*, May–July 1974.

the true nature of the mechanism in which they feel caught. Like Beckett's clowns, Osborne's music-hall entertainer, Pinter's caretaker, Mercer's morally confused minister, Flint, and Orton's faithful retainer, they are the pathetic but touching remnants of a broken system. Dislodged from history, even in the act of recognizing their own insignificance, their own inability to control events, they nonetheless assert a vestigial identity which they hold up against the flux of events. Even if their own identity is disintegrating or scarcely exists (as is clearly the case with Rosencrantz and Guildenstern), they still pit their wounded psyches against a world which they despair of understanding. And because the world which exists indistinctly and threateningly just beyond the focus of their vision is a brutal and uncompassionate one, the remnants of individuality which they can scrape together from the detritus of their hopes and fears make them heroes, ironical and inadequate, but heroes nonetheless in a world which is presented as systematic and logical but devoid of moral purpose.

Yet there is a problem here since in his first play he is drawn to both comedy and farce; the one implying a world in which values exist, the other an antinomian world of ethical relativity. In the former world, heroes, even those who can only deploy a 'tattered dignity', may not only survive but in doing so imply the survival of certain moral principles; in the latter the most they can do is inhabit an autonomous world of their own creation. In *Enter a Free Man* he tries to have it both ways. The title is of course ambiguous. By all external standards George Riley is not free. He survives on hand-outs from his own daughter, and his self-confidence is a fragile product of his family's compassion. But, in another sense, he is free. His imagination and self-respect survive repeated blows. He resists social pressure. And yet, though Stoppard seems to be celebrating his self-sufficiency and his odd-ball courage, he is shown as inhabiting a genuine social environment replete with real psychological problems. Where Willy Loman sustained his illusions precisely because of the social pressures to which he was submitted, George Riley recognizes no social obligations at all. He inhabits his own 'definitely odd' world and thus the psychological and social realism of other sections of the play seem not merely irrelevant but fragments of a different work. Willy Loman could arguably have been a different man in other circumstances. He, too, wanted to make things, but in his case this was to establish a real identity in a world which dealt only in images. If George Riley had been a different man, if he had moved back into the moral world, he would have disappeared. His illogic is his prime virtue; it is his defence against the world.

Stoppard began work on *Rosencrantz and Guildenstern are Dead* in 1964. During a five-month stay in Berlin on a Ford Foundation grant he wrote a one-act Shakespearian pastiche in blank verse. On his return he re-wrote it, abandoning verse for prose, and it was duly performed by the Oxford Drama Group as a 'fringe' production at the Edinburgh Festival in 1966. Following favourable reviews it was subsequently staged by the National Theatre Company in London.

Few writers can have been accorded such instant recognition. Harold Hobson, in *The Sunday Times*, described it as 'the most important event in the British professional theatre of the last nine years'; in other words the most important event since Osborne's *Look Back in Anger* had supposedly changed the direction of British drama. *The Observer* endorsed this view, calling it 'the most brilliant début of the sixties'.

A play which seemed to combine the brittle wit of Oscar Wilde with the mordant humour of Samuel Beckett, *Rosencrantz and Guildenstern are Dead* takes as its main characters two of literature's most marginal figures, attendant lords who, as several critics pointed out, are actually excluded from some productions of *Hamlet*. Stoppard himself has said that, 'the chief object and objective was to exploit a situation which seemed to me to have enormous dramatic and comic potential—of these two guys who in Shakespeare's context don't really know what they are doing. The little they are told is mainly lies, and there's no reason to suppose that they ever find out why they are killed'. 'And', as he points out, 'probably more in the early 1960s than at any other time, that would strike a young playwright as being a perfectly good thing to explore.'

These two 'bewildered innocents' act out a scenario which

they cannot understand, uncertain of their own roles and increasingly disturbed by the apparent meaninglessness of their own lives. Though aware that 'the only beginning is birth and the only end is death', they are forced to believe that there is some purpose in their existence or capitulate to a growing sense of terror. Like the Players who are to perform before Hamlet, they act out their assigned roles with diminishing confidence as they begin to suspect that life lacks both a transcendent dimension and an enabling logic. As the Player says,

'We're actors . . . We pledged our identities, secure in the conventions of our trade that someone would be watching. And then, gradually, no one was. We were caught high and dry . . . Even the habit and stubborn trust that our audience spied upon us from behind the nearest bush, forced our bodies to blunder on long after they had emptied of meaning, until like runaway carts they dragged to a halt. No one came forward. No one shouted at us. The silence was unbreakable, it imposed itself upon us; it was obscene.'

The theatrical metaphor is the dominant one in the play. The pointless prospect of actors without an audience expands to incorporate mankind in general. This is not a disordered world to be restored to consonance by self-sacrifice and heroic action; it is an arbitrary existence in which resolute action decays into mere performance. As Guildenstern observes, 'We don't question . . . we don't doubt . . . we perform.' The chief problem becomes the need to survive from moment to moment without succumbing to panic.

The strategies which they adopt in the face of this situation are familiar enough, particularly to audiences aware of Beckett's *Waiting for Godot*. They blot out their incipient terror by playing Wittgensteinian language games,[1] flipping coins, conversing, reaching out to one another for momentary contact. They attempt to discover pattern and purpose in their existence by use of scientific logic. But all these defences crumble. The language games lead them to real and disturbing questions about their own identity, the coins persistently and alarmingly come down heads every time in

[1] See Ludwig Wittgenstein's *Philosophical Investigations*.

defiance of the laws of chance, and conversation drains away until Guildenstern shouts out in despair, 'Do you think conversation is going to help us now?' Logic is similarly ineffectual, for though Guildenstern asserts that 'the scientific approach to the examination of phenomena is a defence against the pure emotion of fear', the logical explanations which he laboriously constructs collapse under their own weight.

They are caught, then; trapped inside a play which they did not write and doomed to enact roles which they can never understand, lacking as they do vital clues as to the meaning of the total drama. Yet even the autonomous identity of the supposed author of that play is cast in doubt when Rosencrantz anachronistically recalls the famous analogy for the law of probability, whereby, given time, six monkeys typing at random could produce the entire works of Shakespeare. In other words the whole scenario may be simply the consequence of chance and not the ordered product of an omniscient creator. The metaphysical implications are obvious.

They are forced to conclude that the only freedom they possess is that of sailors on a ship, free to move around on the vessel but unable to influence the wind and current which draw them inexorably onwards. Or, more bleakly, it is the freedom to exist in a coffin, aware that one day the lid will be screwed down but able in the meantime to breathe, converse, exist. As Rosencrantz suggests, 'Life in a box is better than no life at all. I expect. You'd have a chance at least. You could lie there thinking—well, at least I'm not dead! In a minute someone's going to bang on the lid and tell me to come out.' This is the last resort: illusion, willed self-deceit of the kind Edward Albee had indicted in *Tiny Alice*. But even this cannot be sustained. When Guildenstern tries to convince himself that 'We are not restricted. No boundaries have been defined, no inhibitions imposed . . . We can breathe. We can relax. We can do what we like or say what we like to whomever we like, without restriction', Rosencrantz adds the necessary and deflating proviso, 'Within limits, of course'.

And as confidence drains away, as the ship, literal and metaphoric, nears its destination, so the defensive illusions begin to disintegrate, flake by flake. Language itself begins to collapse. Freud saw speech not as a path to truth, as a means of destroying barriers between individuals, but as a means of holding truth at bay, of evading the vulnerability which is a necessary corollary of communication. This, indeed, is how Rosencrantz and Guildenstern deploy it. But as the terror of their situation becomes more and more compelling, so this membrane between themselves and truth becomes permeable. The tissue begins to dissolve, and their loss of control is mirrored in a fragmentation of their language.

> ROS: I want to go home.
> GUIL: Don't let them confuse you.
> ROS: I'm out of my step here—
> GUIL: We'll soon be home and high—dry and home—I'll—
> ROS: It's all over my *depth*—
> GUIL:—I'll hie you home and—
> ROS:—out of my head—
> GUIL:—dry you high and—
> ROS (*cracking, high*):—over my step over my head body! —I tell you it's all stopping to a death, it's boding to a depth, stepping to a head, it's all heading to a dead stop—
> GUIL: (*the nursemaid*): There! . . . and we'll soon be home and dry . . . and *high* and dry . . .

It is essentially the same technique as that used by Harold Pinter in *The Birthday Party*, though here the menace is not objectified. It remains vague, generalized.

The play is full of theatrical references. There are plays within plays within plays, a device which implicitly raises questions about the nature of truth. Apart from the obvious references to *Hamlet*, there are others to Albee ('Good old east' derived from 'good old north' in *The Zoo Story*) and Osborne ('Don't clap too hard. It's a very old world' derived from Archie Rice's rather less metaphysical comment in *The Entertainer*, 'Don't clap. It's a very old building'). We are, indeed, constantly reminded of the unreality of what we are watching. Rosencrantz on several occasions shows awareness of the presence of the audience while the conventions of the stage are repeatedly mocked. The consequence is that the audience is reminded that it too is playing a role, collaborating in the establishment of contingent truths. As the Player reminds us, 'truth is only that which is taken to be true. It's the currency of living. There may be nothing behind it, but it doesn't make any difference so long as it is honoured. One acts on assumptions.' It is, in fact, precisely the existence of a world in which the only fixed points are birth and death which creates the need for fictions, for self-sustaining pretence; precisely the need for an ordering of experience which sends people to art, whose hermetic structures imply both a sequential code and a sustainable set of values. The willing suspension of disbelief thus applies not merely to the content of a work but to the assumptions about form, causality and moral progress which have been corollaries of liberal art. Absurdist drama is thus not merely a rejection of liberal convictions about society and the nature of man, it is an implicit critique of the role ascribed to the artist. For he is no less a clown than Vladimir and Estragon;[1] his audience is, for the duration of the play, in a temporal void as real as that occupied by Rosencrantz and Guildenstern and as pathetically dedicated to 'passing the time' while awaiting with absolute faith, like the absurdist characters which they observe, for structure to cohere into meaning.

Nor can one feel that Rosencrantz and Guildenstern's fate derives from their unique position as marginal individuals. For, as we discover, marginality is a matter of focus. In this play Hamlet is marginal, and if the two attendant lords face imminent death, this is no less than faces Hamlet, Polonius, Gertrude, Ophelia and Laertes. Hamlet's observations while holding Yorick's skull contain the essence of Stoppard's play, for it is precisely the existence of the grave which retrospectively deprives life of meaning. As Hamlet observes, what is the meaning of a beauty which simply conceals the skull; what the purpose of humour if it merely cloaks the black comedy of death? Yet such questions pursued too far lead to genuine madness, and having mocked passion and justified inaction, Hamlet acts with vigour and by doing so not merely restores a secular order but reanimates the concept of order itself. This is not true of the world which Rosencrantz and Guilderstern inhabit. Here there is no

---

[1] The two central characters in Samuel Beckett's *Waiting for Godot*.

definable truth, no established pattern, no tradition of morality to be pursued. Their individual qualities are irrelevant to their plight. One is intellectual, incisive, disturbed; the other obtuse, contented, placid. One is a leader; the other is led. It makes no difference. Such characteristics cannot alter their plight. Consequently they display an alarming uncertainty as to their identities, and as the pressure on them increases, so they exchange roles, thus emphasizing that these are indeed roles, assumed modes of action generated by the exigencies of situation rather than by the compulsions of authentic character.

Is Stoppard, then, an absurdist? Like most arbitrary categories this is frequently more misleading than helpful, as has proved the case with writers such as Pinter and Albee. Yet the iconography of *Rosencrantz and Guildenstern are Dead* is familiar to audiences who cut their critical teeth on Beckett and Ionesco. The absurdists captured a deracinated world—a world in which the potential for action and communication has been irrevocably eroded. The setting is timeless, the landscape an expressionistic desert reminiscent of Dali's lapidary wilderness[1] or the claustrophobic living room of modern, uncommunal living. The capacity for action is minimal and ironic. Language itself is simply an elaborate papering over of cracks, which constantly threaten to open up beneath those who remain either blithely unaware of their plight or numbed with despair. That anguish obviously exists in Stoppard's play—a work in which two men are seen 'passing the time in a place without any visible character', clinging fiercely to the conviction that they 'have not been picked out... simply to be abandoned', that they are 'entitled to some direction', only to confess at the end of their 'play' that 'it is not enough. To be told so little—to such an end—and still, finally, to be denied an explanation.' The only resources available to these abandoned characters are the compassion with which they respond to one another and the humour which they deploy as a means of neutralizing their fear. Niebur's comment that laughter is a kind of no man's land between faith and despair is clearly applicable to

[1] The adjective refers to Dali's paintings, which often picture desolate landscapes, dominated by rocks and stones.

Rosencrantz and Guildenstern are Dead. For Rosencrantz and Guildenstern themselves, humour is a means of preserving sanity; for Stoppard it is a natural product of disjunction—of the gulf between cause and effect, aspiration and fulfilment, word and meaning, which is the root alike of pain, absurdity, and laughter, and a clue to the relativity of truth, itself a subject to which Stoppard has repeatedly returned.

Stoppard has said that, 'What I try to do is to end up by contriving the perfect marriage between the play of ideas and farce or, perhaps, even high comedy . . . to that end I have been writing plays which are farcical and without an idea in their funny heads, and I have also written plays which are all mouth . . . and don't bring off the comedy. And occasionally, I think *Jumpers* would be an example, I've got fairly close to a play which works as a funny play and which makes coherent, in terms of theatre, a fairly complicated intellectual argument.'[1] While it is true that the argument behind *Rosencrantz and Guildenstern are Dead* is not complex, its strength lies precisely in the skill with which he has blended humour with metaphysical enquiry, the success with which he has made the play's theatricality an essential element of its thematic concern. It is, indeed, a kind of *Waiting for Godot*, in which Vladimir and Estragon become university wits.

Yet, as he indicates above, not all of his plays have such serious aspirations, and Stoppard followed *Rosencrantz and Guildenstern are Dead* and *Enter A Free Man* with two adroit and well-constructed works (*The Real Inspector Hound* and *After Magritte*), whose chief fascination resides in the skill with which he unravels his own aesthetic conundrums. As he has said, '*After Magritte* and *The Real Inspector Hound* are short plays and they really are an attempt to bring off a sort of comic coup in pure mechanistic terms. They were *conceived* as short plays.'

The ostensible subject of *The Real Inspector Hound* is the rivalry between two drama critics who, somewhat bewilderingly, are drawn into the action of the play which they are reviewing. But we have Stoppard's warning that 'the one thing *The Real Inspector Hound* isn't about, as far as I am concerned, is theatre critics . . . I just got into it, and I knew that I

[1] 'Ambushes for the Audience', *Theatre Quarterly*, May–July 1974.

wanted it somehow to resolve itself in a breathtakingly neat, complex and utterly comprehensible way.' He does, admittedly, give free rein to his considerable talents as a parodist, mocking both the conventions of antiquated drawing-room whodunnits and the critical styles of drama reviewers (Birdboot works for a popular paper: 'let us give thanks and double thanks for a good clean show without a trace of smut'; Moon writes for a rather more pretentious readership: '*Je suis*, it seems to be saying, *ergo sum* . . . and here one is irresistibly reminded of Voltaire's cry, *Voilà!*'). But once again he is concerned with raising more fundamental questions about the nature of truth and theatricality, though no longer with the same degree of seriousness which he had brought to his first successful play. Once again he creates a play within a play, the audience, by a trick of the eye, being projected into the play which they are watching, as the two critics themselves will be later in the work. The opening stage direction indicates that 'the audience appear to be confronted by their own reflection in a huge mirror'. In many ways the play is struck from the same die as *Rosencrantz and Guildenstern are Dead*. Birdboot, like Rosencrantz, is a literal-minded man whose reach does not extend beyond his grasp. Metaphysics disturb him and he retains his grip on reality by reducing all experience to banalities. Moon, on the other hand, is reminiscent of Guildenstern. He sees significance in everything and is dominated by a growing sense of his own insecurity. Yet, however they may differ, both find themselves occupying the same stage, desperately trying to understand what they are doing, cast suddenly and without appeal in a second-rate drama.

Critics have inevitably invoked the name of Pirandello in relation to Stoppard's work, and there is, indeed, considerable similarity in their concern with the nature of reality, the relativity of truth and the fluid nature of identity. Both writers have repeatedly resorted to the theatrical metaphor in expressing the conviction that individual existence consists of a number of overlapping roles, that appearance and reality are inevitably and instructively divorced from one another and that life is more usefully regarded as a series of improvisations than as the acting out of a prepared scenario. Nor is it without significance that the play which Birdfoot and Moon are reviewing is a whodunnit, the supreme example of rational art which, particularly in the parody version which Stoppard offers us, derives its whole effect from the conviction that individuals are justifiably identified with their roles (victim, murderer, detective), indeed gain their meaning purely in terms of the part which they play in a highly structured scenario. It is also a form which rests on the conviction that reality is susceptible of rational analysis, since it turns so clearly on causality. But, as a character in *Jumpers* remarks, 'Unlike mystery novels, life does not guarantee a dénouement.' Thus, when the prepared text is suddenly disturbed, when the hapless reviewers find themselves on stage, these conventions are threatened. Stoppard then offers his audience a difficult choice in that in order to restore a sense of order, to maintain the conventions, to avoid the conviction that the action has become irrational, arbitrary and improvised, it is forced to accept a number of wholly absurd assumptions; it is placed, in other words, in the position of Rosencrantz and Guildenstern who are forced for their own peace of mind to presume the paradigmatic nature of theatre, to accept the conviction that performance at all levels implies the existence of an audience.

The Real Inspector Hound is not a wholly satisfactory play. It is more adroit than it is convincing. The parody, though at times brilliant, is too often facile; the metaphysical dimension, deliberately underplayed, is nonetheless too often sacrificed to the witty remark. A confessedly light-weight comedy, the play finally stops annoyingly short of examining the implications of its central premise.

It is not surprising to learn that Magritte is Stoppard's favourite artist, for both men secure their particular effects by essentially the same method. The wrenching of object from setting, of event from context, results not merely in a revealing absurdity but in a perception of the contingent nature of truth. But Stoppard is no surrealist. The *tableau* at the beginning of his one-act play, *After Magritte*, is not a surrealist image designed to liberate the imagination, to energize the subconscious, but a teasing problem in logic, a conundrum to be unravelled. Its metaphorical significance remains largely unexamined, but as Stoppard himself commented, it is 'not an intellectual play, it's a nuts-and-bolts comedy'.

The play opens with an old woman lying prone on an ironing board with her foot resting against an iron and with a bowler hat on her stomach. Of the two other people in the room one is dressed for ballroom dancing and the other, a man equipped with thigh-length waders, is apparently trying to blow out an electric light bulb. The remaining furniture is piled against the front door and a policeman is staring through the window. The play itself consists of an elaborate explanation for this apparently absurd situation. It is an adroit demonstration of the fact that truth is a matter of perspective. As one of the characters observes, 'there is obviously a perfectly logical explanation for everything'. Yet though logic does indeed hold, as it does in the radio plays *Albert's Bridge* and *If You're Glad I'll be Frank*, it has no connexion with the inner life of his characters. As George remarks in *Jumpers*, 'if rationality were the criterion for things being allowed to exist, the world would be one gigantic field of soya beans! The irrational, the emotional, the whimsical . . . these are the stamp of humanity which makes reason a civilizing force. In a wholly rational society the moralist will be a variety of crank. . . .' As a consequence these shorter plays are little more than five-finger exercises, displays of virtuoso talent which hint at a metaphysical dimension which they forbear to examine. The same could not be said of his more recent work.

Stoppard has said that *Jumpers* was the first play in which he specifically set out to 'ask a question and try to answer it, or at any rate put the counter question'. And though once again he chooses a comic framework, the question is a serious one and one moreover which leads on to the more avowedly political questions of *Travesties*. It is a play about the growingly materialist base of modern society and the desperate attempt by its protagonist to establish the existence and reality of transcendent values.

His protagonist, another bewildered individual assailed by authority and threatened by the positivist assumptions of his society, struggles manfully to establish by logical means the existence of moral absolutes and the credibility of God. As Professor of Moral Philosophy he tries to oppose the rationalist assumptions of his age by deploying a blend of intuitionist philosophy, deductive reasoning, and empirical evidence. He does so, however, in the most unpromising circumstances. The radical liberal party have just won an election and have begun the process of rationalizing society by appointing a veterinary surgeon as Archbishop of Canterbury. A British moonlanding, itself a victory for technology, has ended in near disaster, the captain pragmatically abandoning his companion in order to return to the equally pragmatic earth. And his wife, Dotty, a well-known singer, who may or may not have murdered the Professor of Logic, has retired from show business, her lyrical invocations to the moon effectively destroyed not merely by an antinomian science which daily appropriates further aspects of human experience, but by a perspective which suddenly reduces human significance. As she explains,

'it's all over now. Not only are we no longer the still centre of God's universe, we're not even uniquely graced by his footprint in man's image . . . Man is on the moon, his feet on solid ground, and he has seen us whole . . . and all our absolutes . . . that seemed to be the very condition of our existence, how did *they* look to two moonmen . . . Like the local customs of another place.'

All George's convictions seem to be invalidated by events. As he tries to construct his logical defence of illogic and substantiate his faith in a non-relativistic ethic, a group of acrobatic philosophers are busily engaged in disposing of the corpse of one of their colleagues—a logician who has come to doubt the morality of his own denial of moral values. Even the language which he uses subverts his intention, since it too is relativistic, a pragmatic approximation. He is, in other words, in an absurd situation building logical structures as flawed as those of the bewildered George Riley in *Enter A Free Man*. Yet he and Dotty remain dedicated not merely to humane values but to preserving an element of mystery in a society which regards human experience as wholly classifiable in rational terms. As he confesses,

'When I push *my* convictions to absurdity, I arrive at God. . . . All I know is that I think that I know that I know that nothing can be created out of nothing, that my moral conscience is different from the rules of my tribe, and that there is more in me than meets the microscope—and because of that I'm lumbered with this incredible, indescribable and definitely shifty *God*, the trump card of atheism.'

The irony of his situation, however, resides in the fact that while he elaborates his defence of values, in the admittedly somewhat limited privacy of his own study, the world outside is renouncing all interest in the matter. Engaged only on a theoretical level, he implicitly compounds the forces which he deplores. Just as life inevitably evades his attempt to pin it down with words, his elaborate arguments sliding off into anecdote and parenthetical by-ways, so his grasp on the real world is seen to be tenuous at best. Obsessed with validating an abstraction, he fails to grasp the totalitarian nature of the forces which have just come to power, blinded, ironically, by their use of the word 'liberal'. That he succeeds iconically in destroying his own over-elaborate proofs when he kills the rabbit and crushes the tortoise with which he had planned to clinch his rational justification of irrationality, is evidence of his own ironic contradictions. As Dotty suggests, he is 'living in dreamland'. Indeed, the final scene of the play is presented in what Stoppard calls 'bizarre dream form'. It consists of the symposium for which George has been preparing himself throughout the rest of the play. Following a parodied and semi-coherent statement of a materialist view of man by the decidedly materialist and incidentally lecherous Vice-Chancellor, the new secular Archbishop of Canterbury is summoned. Though himself an atheist, he proceeds to imitate Thomas Becket and voices the opinion, heretical in a rational state, that 'surely belief in man could find room for man's beliefs'. When he is consequently murdered for this affront to rationality and political expediency, George fails to intervene, unwilling to make the necessary connexion between theory and practice. He simply excuses his detachment by asserting that 'that seems to be a political quarrel . . . Surely only a proper respect for absolute values . . . universal truths . . . *philosophy*—'. His desperate desire to get the conversation back onto an abstract plane is interrupted by a gun shot, as the Archbishop is deftly removed from the human pyramid into which the gymnastic philosophers had carefully incorporated him. Unmoved, George launches into his prepared text on the existence of moral values only to be interrupted again, this time finally, by the Vice-Chancellor. He, in turn, glibly outlines a pragmatic defence of a positivist stance which, in its justification for baseless optimism over the plight of modern man, ironically applies not only to the radical liberals intent on eradicating an inefficient individualism but also to George. For he, in turn, is so caught up in his own confident assertions of moral values that he fails to see the collapse of everything which gives those values meaning. This society is nothing if not pragmatic. The police force seems likely to be 'thinned out to a ceremonial front for the peace-keeping activities of the Army', while the Chair of Divinity at the university no longer invites applicants and can be offered as a bribe to an over-inquisitive policeman or as a reward for a particularly diligent porter. Against such a situation George's confused liberalism seems no defence. His convictions seem paradoxically to lead him to contradiction and equivocation. His respect for reason leads him to attempt a rational justification for faith, while his commitment to tolerance makes him endorse the very forces which threaten his philosophy most directly. 'It would be presumptuous' he says, 'to condemn radical ideas simply because they appear to me to be self-evidently stupid and criminal, if they do happen to be at the same time radical.' His passion is deflected into his work, into finding the right word, the right image, into creating a convincing structure. In many ways his problem is that of the playwright himself, in love with words and ideas, but detached from the real world by virtue of his craft, as the philosopher is by virtue of his need to deal in abstractions rather than concrete realities. At any rate this question became central to his later work, *Travesties*, which attempts to examine the whole question of the role of the artist.

George inevitably fails in his attempt to prove the existence of God, as he does in his effort to establish the absolute nature of moral values. His convictions remain nothing more than an expression of faith disguised as logical inferences. But, after all, as the wholly irrational relationship between George and Dotty would seem to suggest, 'the irrational, the emotional, the whimsical . . . are the stamp of humanity which makes reason a civilizing force'. The anarchic energy of this embattled couple, alarmed as they are by the threatened collapse of their world but resisting with sporadic displays of affection, humour and faith, contrasts sharply with the crudely rational world which intrudes on the television screen and in the pointless precision with which the philosophical jumpers turn their literal and metaphorical somersaults. As George remarks, 'now and again, not necessarily in the contemplation of polygons or new-born babes, nor in the extremities of pain or joy, but more probably in some quite trivial moment, it seems to me that life itself is the mundane figure which argues perfection at its limiting curve.' And if perfection is in fact unreachable, the existence of such moments is enough to justify the faith and lyrical yearnings of George and his vulnerable wife.

The real advance in *Jumpers* is not merely that Stoppard succeeds in fusing a comic approach with metaphysics, but that he begins to control the resources of theatre with greater confidence and skill than before. The philosophical acrobats, performing their various contortions and constructing human pyramids, constitute a perfect image of the intellectual processes which they enact. The huge television screen which projects the external world into the phrenetic private life of the Moores is both an assertion of that connexion between public and private morality which Stoppard is anxious to establish, and itself evidence of an alienating technology. Even the word-games, the ambiguities, the puns, which are all recognizable marks of Stoppard's work, are entirely functional in a play which is in large part concerned with the inadequacy of attempts to capture reality with words, the palpable absurdity of measuring with a rule whose length obstinately varies from moment to moment. The apparent absurdity of the opening scene during which a stripper flies across the stage on a trapeze, Dotty flounders her way through a bewildering medley of 'moon' songs, and the yellow uniformed gymnasts perform their feats until the death of one of their number precipitates an abrupt end, resembles the bizarre opening of *After Magritte*. Indeed, as in that play, these impossibly incongruous elements are shown to be capable of a perfectly rational explanation; but whereas in the earlier work Stoppard was largely content with his display of ingenuity, here the unravelling of confusions is endemic to the style and purpose of the play's protagonist. And though once again it becomes apparent that events can be shown to sustain a logical explanation, the simple unravelling of that logic leaves a residual problem, since it can offer no explanation for the irrational yearnings which torture both Dotty and George but which, it is increasingly apparent, are seen by Stoppard as constituting the essence of human nature, the core of individual resistance to reification.

The moral dimension of Stoppard's work appears at times to suffer from his own commitment to farce. He seems afraid to take himself seriously, to allow his humour to become a consistent critique—hence his *penchant* for parody rather than satire, his technique of building scenes through contradiction. As he once remarked, 'I write plays because dialogue is the most respectable way of contradicting myself.'

It follows that he feels 'committed art' to be 'a kind of bogus exercise'. As he has explained, 'I get deeply embarrassed by the statements and postures of "committed" theatre. There is no such thing as "pure" art—art is a commentary on something else in life—it might be adultery in the suburbs, or the Vietnamese war. I think that art ought to involve itself in contemporary social and political history as much as anything else, but I find it deeply embarrassing when large claims are made for such an involvement: when, because art takes notice of something important, it's claimed that the art is important. It's not.'

Travesties attempts to debate essentially this problem. As Stoppard has said, 'it puts the question in a more extreme form. It asks whether an artist has to justify himself in political terms *at all*', 'whether the words "revolutionary" and "artist" are capable of being synonymous or whether they are mutually exclusive, or something in between.' It is a play which brings together the opposite extremes of the debate in the persons of James Joyce, whom Stoppard elsewhere quotes as saying that the history of Ireland, troubles and all, was justified because it led to a book such as *Ulysses*, and Lenin, who felt that the only justification for art lay in its political utility. Mediating between the two is Tristan Tzara, drawn simultaneously in both directions; on the one hand spinning neologisms and cascades of words like Joyce, convinced that the artist constitutes the difference between brute existence and any sense of transcendence, and on the other seeing the writer as the conscience of the Revolution and justifying the brutality of its servants. However, the question is effectively begged by the form in which Stoppard chooses to conduct the debate. For the most part we see the characters only as they are refracted through the febrile imagination of a minor British consular official, Henry Carr. Just as *Hamlet*, viewed through the eyes of Rosencrantz and Guildenstern, is drained of tragic meaning, so too this clash of ideas loses much of its urgency seen from the perspective of a deluded, prejudiced and erratic minor functionary. In this context, perforce, they become mere performers in a Wildean comedy which jolts along with all the manic energy and manifest dishonesty of a bogus memoir.

In 'The Critic as Artist', Oscar Wilde remarks of memoirs that they are 'generally written by people who have either entirely lost their memories, or have never done anything worth remembering'. This proves all too accurate a description of Carr's memoirs, which tend to confuse his own fictions with those of *The Importance of Being Earnest* in which he had once scored a minor success. Indeed, apart from appropriating dialogue and even two of his characters directly from Wilde's play, he even restructures history so that it conforms to the requirements of high comedy. The title is thus an appropriate one as Stoppard, through Carr, presents a travesty of both literary styles and historical events.

Carr erroneously remembers himself as having been British Consul in Zurich during the First World War, at a time when Lenin, Joyce and Tzara were living out an expatriate existence, plotting their various revolutions in art and society. In juxtaposing these forces, Stoppard seems to be suggesting that history is no less a fiction than Joyce's parodic constructions; that it has no more logic than Tzara's poems, which are themselves the product of pure chance. But something about this equation of literary performance and *bravura* politics fails to convince. In picking Lenin as the embodiment of political fabulism, he engages not merely a historically bound figure who can be parodied as himself a none too competent role player, but also a palpable reality whose particular fictions have assumed an implacable form. There is a degree, therefore, to which Stoppard seems to have been unnerved by the ineluctable consequences of revolutionary conviction. We know, or think that we know, that the opinions expressed by the various characters in the play are those which Carr constructs. The single exception is Lenin, who stands, perhaps, as a corrective to those fictions—massive, real. The grand claims of Tzara, the self-confident assertiveness of Joyce, real or illusory, can only inhabit a world defined by the prosaic realities defined by Lenin. The massive scale of his impact on history, an impact which transcends both the banality of his life-style and his literary style, is a fact tucked away in the mind of the audience. Just as his presence seems to neutralize the play's anarchic humour, to inhibit the irresponsible contempt for social realities, so his presence in the real world does much the same. He is a materialist and the material has no time for fantasy as Dotty had realized in *Jumpers*. The details of Lenin's career, solemnly narrated by Nadya, his Russian secretary (a narration which Stoppard incautiously invites his directors to edit to taste) contrasts markedly with the anarchic frivolity of those other revolutionaries who surround him in Zurich, and whose revolutions are contained by the boundaries of artistic concern.

From his initial description of the characters through to Lenin's departure for Russia, it is the political activist alone who for the most part escapes parody. Carr's imagination makes both Joyce and Tzara perform a series of bizzarre antics. Indeed they become the chief actors in a baroque farce, likely at any moment to lapse into song and dance. Lenin remains stolidly detached. His speeches are authentic, a point which Stoppard is at pains to stress. He is the only character, in other words, who is not controlled by Carr's distorting imagination, though according to the conventions of the play he too should be moulded to fit the elderly diplomat's psychic needs. And though this is perhaps a conscious comment on the nature of the difference between the artist and the social revolutionary, a difference which makes the fusion of the two roles unlikely, it also has the effect of dislocating the play. The second act is not merely less funny than the first, containing a detailed documentary account of Lenin's career (accompanied by objectifying photographs), and also a debate about the role of the artist between Carr on the one hand and Tzara and Cecily on the other; it is also less effective. The sources for the first act are Wilde's play, *The Importance of Being Earnest*, James Joyce's *Ulysses* and the documented excesses of Dada; the source for the second is Lenin's biography. The change in mood is inevitable. The result is a curiously reverential treatment of the political leader, an approach quite at odds with the tone of a play which seems to suggest his poverty of imagination, his disregard for moral values and his misconceptions about the function of art and history. Farce drains away as Stoppard comes to the heart of his concern, and though he is careful to conceal his own commitments by refusing to resolve the contradictory views expressed by his characters, the stylistic dislocation exposes the seriousness of his concern as the play becomes at moments a genuine debate about the importance of being earnest—of adopting a humourless dedication to social realities.

Stoppard has called his distinguishing mark, an 'absolute lack of certainty about almost anything'. This detachment, though unnerving in some respects, gives him the freedom, for most of the time, to criticize the materialist inhumanity of Lenin, the spurious artistic arrogance of Joyce, the cavalier socialism of Tzara and the aristocratic hauteur of Carr. All seem squarely rooted in self-concern. But Stoppard's detachment slips once or twice. Despite his failure to locate a satisfactory mode of parody with regard to Lenin, his distrust of ideologists surfaces at moments, cutting through the comic banter which otherwise for the most part defuses any attempt at moral seriousness. Carr's rebuttal of Marxist analysis and Cecily's disingenuous justification for Lenin's inhumanity are too studied to sustain a credible commitment to ethical distance. The assumptions of farce come up against the moral presumptions of comedy, and the resulting clash disturbs not merely stylistic unity but also the momentum of the humour.

In a conflict between a materialist view of history and an approach which translates the substantial realities of human life into fictions, fantasies, and plots, there can be little doubt where Stoppard's sympathies will lie—nor, by the end, can we be in any doubt that these two views are so clearly antithetical that the notion of a revolutionary artist is a demonstrable contradiction in terms. Yet, in his own way, Carr is as dedicated to a simplistic view of reality as is Lenin. He wants to believe in a world in which he can play a central role. Language must provide a precise symbolism, the artist must be a beautifier of reality, a licenced hedonist. He resists reality with as much dedication as either Joyce or Tzara. He is, of course, in a real sense a playwright. He 'creates' the drama in which he casts himself as the central character (as, essentially, does each individual). He claims the same right to refuse social liability as he believes the true artist must do. As he remarks,

'to be an artist *at all* is like living in Switzerland during a world war'.

In this respect, also, he is close kin to Rosencrantz and Guildenstern, to George Riley and Professor Moore. Like Stoppard himself, these characters choose to respond to the bewildering vagaries of existence by creating games, plays, by remaking the world until its absurdities dissolve in simple performance. Lenin, Joyce, Tzara, Carr, all are equally pathetic and heroic as they inhabit with such apparent conviction the fictions which they choose to regard as reality. Role players all, they seek to construct plots which will make sense of their urge for personal, social or metaphysical order. Art, politics, philosophy, logic are deployed with varying degrees of conviction. But behind it all there lurks the savage joke which is implicit in the figure of the ageing Carr who reconstructs his past out of the same compulsions which led Beckett's Krapp to turn the switch of his tape recorder to replay the hopes and aspirations of his youth. It is Carr's distinction that he glimpses this truth for a moment and is still able to justify his challenge to reality.

Stoppard's subsequent plays have marked something of a shift in his work, or at least an intensification of his desire to validate a moral view of the world. *Every Good Boy Deserves Favour* (1977) is a play written for six characters and an entire symphony orchestra. It was inspired by an invitation from André Previn, then principal conductor of the London Symphony Orchestra, and owed its subject—the Soviet treatment of dissidents—to his own increasing concern and to the research which he was conducting for the television play which was eventually to become *Professional Foul*.

Alexander Ivanov is imprisoned in a Soviet mental hospital for protesting against the arrest of fellow dissidents. His namesake, an authentic madman, who believes himself to be in charge of an orchestra, shares his cell. The situation is further complicated by the fact that there is also a genuine orchestra in which Alexander's doctor is a minor player, as he is in the state apparatus of which the orchestra is an image.

Embarrassed by Alexander's hunger strike, the authorities try to persuade him to capitulate, first through torture, and then by urging his son, Sacha, to convince him. But he persists in being out of tune with the state. Finally anxious to get him off his hands, his psychiatrist, who, while regrettably lacking in psychiatric qualifications, combines the unlikely roles of KGB colonel and professor of linguistics, deliberately mistakes the two prisoners for one another and releases them both.

The play is a subtle work in which the debate between the rights of the individual and the rules of the state are reflected visually and aurally in the contrast between the monologues of the solitary prisoner and the harmonies of the anonymous orchestra. But the play's humour emerges from a debate over the nature of reality, a problem equally acute in a mental hospital in which one's 'opinions are your symptoms', and a state in which reality is a matter of state doctrine. Thus, when Alexander's doctor insists that they must all 'act together' he is saying no more than the literal truth about a society in which fictions must be solemnly enacted as realities.

The black American writer, Richard Wright, once told of an occasion on which the Communist cell of which he was a member was thrown into a paroxysm of mutual denunciation at the instigation of what the members all took to be a member of the Party hierarchy. Eventually, they discovered that he had in fact escaped from a local mental hospital. This is essentially the conceit which Stoppard employs here, since sanity becomes a function of state decree and reality a prescribed fiction. Clearly, the whole hospital/prison is indeed involved in an act, as is the society beyond its walls. And the dissonant note is a threat which must be suppressed in appearance if not in fact, whether or not the orchestra/state is controlled by a madman. Thus, the debate over whether Alexander's room should be described as a ward or a cell contains the essence of the political confrontation.

And it is an inevitable consequence of such a system that the distinction between warder and prisoner, doctor and patient, teacher and pupil, is eroded. They are all trapped inside fictions, while the denial of reality is an article of faith required from all. Thus the dissident voice challenges not only authority but a definition of the real.

Alexander's resistance is echoed by his son, Sacha, whose violent and deliberately undisciplined playing of the triangle in his school orchestra is a reflection of his father's refusal to conform and, ironically, of the madman, Ivanov, who likewise plays the triangle in his fantasy orchestra. But Sacha himself is the source of a minor problem in the play. For there is obviously a considerable potential for sentimentality in the plight of a young boy deprived of his father—a not illegitimate intimation of the human cost of political hubris. But the effect is, at times, too easily won, more so on the stage than on the page. And though Stoppard seeks to deflect the plunge into simple pathos by having the boy's appeals sung rather than spoken, he is not always successful.

By the same token, the play's strategy, to grant moral primacy to the real, is, on occasion, at odds with more subtle questions about the nature of that reality and the processes of authentication. It is, indeed, out of this tension that the play's ambiguous ending derives. For Alexander is released into a society which remains unchanged, and though he and Sacha stand apart from the orchestra, which all the other characters have now joined, his son's invocation, 'Papa, don't be crazy!/Everything can be all right!', is finely balanced between hope and irony, the child remaining committed to his father but echoing the language of the state.

The absurdist world of *Rosencrantz and Guildenstern Are Dead* was clearly as invulnerable to ethical commitment as it was to ideology. Irony was generated not by the gulf between appearance and reality but by their coincidence. In *Every Good Boy Deserves Favour* there is an observable truth, no matter what appearance may suggest. But, at the same time, Stoppard does not abandon his concern with theatricality. For if the character of Victor Fainberg, the Soviet dissident, provides some of the material for the figure of Alexander, he appears in the form which Stoppard chooses to give him. Indeed, when Vladimir Bukowsky, who is, in a sense, 'the off-stage hero', and who had recently been released to fly to the West, actually turned up in London and attended the play's rehearsal, Stoppard admits that, 'his presence was disturbing. For people working on a piece of theatre,' he suggests, 'terra-firma is a self-contained world even while it mimics the real one. That is the necessary condition of making theatre, and it is also our luxury.' There was, he confesses, 'a sense of worlds colliding.' So that if his liberal impulse no longer permits him totally to undermine the possibility of a reality which can generate morality, as Pirandello had done in *Right You Are (If You Think So)* which similarly plays ironic games with madness and truth, he remains fascinated with the manipulative power of the writer—a power which, paradoxically, allies him with the very forces which he would wish to denounce. The playwright is, after all, as much a manipulator of language as is the philologically qualified KGB colonel, and it is that skill with words which enables both men to achieve their objectives. He, too, generates fictions which his characters must inhabit. He also conducts an orchestra, even though the chord he wishes it to sound may be disruptive of conventional harmonies. The 'luxury' of the playwright is thus potentially the source of guilt, as detachment and verbal facility come to seem morally problematic. And this is a theme which he took up more directly in his next play, *Professional Foul* (1977).

Though written with a rapidity which worries Stoppard—the writer being no less prone than the cleric to associate grace with suffering—*Professional Foul* is a consummate achievement. The plot is squarely concerned with those ethical problems which have increasingly moved to the centre of his work. The action takes place in Prague, where Anderson, the John Stuart Mill Professor of Ethics at Cambridge University, is to deliver a paper on 'Ethical Fictions as Ethical Foundations' to a colloquium of philosophers. His trip is fraught with moral dilemmas, from the trivial to the profound. The fact of a professor of ethics reading a nudie magazine is more ironic than challenging, as is his decision to slip away from the conference to see a football match. But when a former student, Pavel Hollar, asks him to smuggle a manuscript to the West he is confronted with a moral problem which cannot adequately be tackled with a dispassionate logic and a mind more adjusted to arcane debates about the nature of meaning and the function of language than the practical issues of personal freedom, his own and that of others.

His first response to Hollar's request is to see it as vaguely improper. He thus attempts to return the thesis. But on arriving at Hollar's apartment he is detained by the police who are searching for the very document which he has in his briefcase. He does what any professor of ethics would do in the circumstances—he lies, and retreats to his hotel room as soon as he can. But the membrane between abstract morality and practical reality has been destroyed. Thus, instead of delivering his own paper to the colloquium, he lectures on the topic of his student's dissertation, modified by his own new perceptions. And the following day he smuggles the thesis out of the country by placing it in the luggage of one of his colleagues, whose own philosophical stance is so avowedly relativist that the action can scarcely be seen as the dubious moral enterprise which doubtless it is.

The basic strategy of the play is to expose a confident moral philosopher to a genuine ethical dilemma in such a way as to shock him into realising that moral problems operate within the vicious causalities of reality, rather than constituting a kind of game, a subtle play of logic and language. Thus, when he is asked to smuggle the manuscript he at first mistakes the request as a philosophical conundrum, and then refuses on the impeccable grounds that his invitation to speak at the colloquium was 'a contract . . . freely entered into,' which precluded such a deception. The argument is a neat application of the very Lockean principles which lie at the heart of Hollar's thesis. Anderson, pleased with the intellectual neatness of his response, is at first oblivious to the wider implications of his stance. Thus, political dubiety becomes simply an interesting problem in ethics, and when Hollar admits that his assertion of an individual ethic is an 'unsafe conclusion,' Anderson naturally interprets the phrase logically rather than politically.

Indeed, language is shown to be hopelessly plastic. The scope for misunderstanding, a repeated theme of the play, is such that it is difficult to arrive at a system of morality based on the assumption of shared values. So, when Anderson rises to leave the conference and his gesture is misinterpreted as a desire to ask the speaker a question, his response contains an important clue to the play's method. He observes that 'the important truths are simple and monolithic. The essentials for a given situation speak for themselves, and language is as capable of obscuring the truth as of revealing it.' And yet, of course, the very fact of the misunderstanding which leads to the remark, taken with his own repeated failure to 'read' the situation in which he finds himself, would seem to deny its validity.

The truth seems to lie closer to that observed by his boorish fellow conferee, McKendrick. 'There aren't any principles . . . There are only a lot of principled people trying to behave as though there were.' He is similarly correct when

33

he remarks to Anderson that, 'you end up using a moral principle as your excuse for acting against moral interest.' This, after all, is Anderson's 'professional foul.' Like the footballer who deliberately fouls to prevent a goal, Anderson invokes the niceties of ethical principle to avoid acting in a principled way. The professional foul is the wilful suspension of morality in the name of a more proximate ethic.

But, following the shock of his student's arrest, and his awareness of his own instinctive fear and consequent human failure, he reaches conclusions which are essentially those which he offers in his newly-written conference paper—a paper which the chairman sees as such a threat to the system he serves that he arranges for a fake fire alarm to empty the hall. Thus, in his paper, Anderson defines individual rights as 'fictions' which nonetheless act as 'incentives to the adoption of practical values,' and, which, despite their fictive quality, must be treated 'as if they were truths.' So, morality is not a series of absolutes but a search for the principles behind good behaviour. There is, indeed, no ultimate sanction which makes a professional foul unethical, but unless one acts as though there were, it would be impossible to live. Thus, though moral absolutes no longer command belief, a sense of fairness, of right action, still persists. While it may have no warrant in logic or metaphysics and possesses no sanction with which to enforce its presumptions, it is a fiction which proves persistent, potent, and functional. It is, in other words, a pre-verbal conviction which can no more be conclusively demonstrated than can George's God in *Jumpers*.

As he says, 'There is a sense of right and wrong which precedes utterance. It is individually experienced and it concerns one person's dealing with another person. From this we have built a system of ethics which is the sum of individual acts of recognition of individual right.' This is, of course, a long way removed from his earlier position of scrupulous detachment, in which morality was, in effect, a stage on which characters debated the nuances of language and the niceties of logic. But such refinements have been dislodged by a human experience in which moral philosophy has focussed suddenly into a sharp point of personal responsibility. His former scrupulousness now seems an aesthetic rather than an ethical act.

And, of course, such a conclusion is not without its relevance to a playwright whose reputation has come to turn on his facility with language, his command of paradox, his subtle arabesques of logic. The play is, indeed, an articulate playwright's confession of the inadequacy and the deceptive nature of language. Stoppard has increasingly found himself defending a view of moral behaviour which cannot be adequately encompassed in words, nor demonstrated as a function of reason. His response has been to place that dilemma at the heart of his work—to stress the plasticity of language, its lack of innocence. Thus, increasingly, his characters tend to be people whose business is words—philosophers, writers, journalists—but who are trapped in a language which simply cannot contain or express their drive towards a necessary vision of liberal responsibility.

By the same token his jokes have become more integral. Despite his love of the one-liner there is now a reflexive quality about the humour, as misunderstandings, *double entendres* and verbal impasses reveal a language inadequate to the task of explaining man to himself. This is not to say that the humour is not itself in some way redemptive—as it proved to be in *Rosencrantz and Guildenstern Are Dead*. But it is not simply the sugar-coating on a philosophical pill. Nor is he any longer content with the challenge to create perfect mechanical butterflies (*After Magritte*, *The Real Inspector Hound*, *Dirty Linen*). McKendrick's observation that the creation of wit, paradox, and verbal facility is 'an occupation for gentlemen,' is a piece of self-criticism on Stoppard's part as well as an accurate description of Anderson's social, intellectual and moral snobbery.

In *Travesties*, Lenin's utilitarian view of literature becomes prime evidence of his moral failure, as life is subordinated to ideology. And, in his strictly functional world, the newspapers, similarly, have to be cowed in the name of freedom which can only have meaning if the word is distorted by the pressure of an unquestioned conviction. In *Night and Day* (1978) the same point is made in relation to the Western press. Likewise, *Professional Foul* and *Night and Day* are companion pieces—the one examining the ethical problems generated by a closed society, the other, the moral dilemmas of sustaining a supposedly open society.

Stoppard feels passionately about the freedom of the press and strenuously opposes the 'closed-shop' principle, which would exclude everyone but union members from writing for it. Yet, for all that, *Night and Day* is not simply a polemical piece, lightened by the usual display of wit. It recognises not only the triviality of most journalism, but also the self-deception associated with the notion of freedom. The journalist, no less than the writer, is a part of the system which he claims dispassionately to describe; even those who shape reality for others are themselves in turn shaped by that reality.

Night and Day is set in a mythical African country, called Kambawe. Wagner, a Fleet Street journalist, who prides himself on his professionalism, arrives with his photographer, Guthrie, to cover an incipient civil war, only to discover that he has been scooped by Jake Milne, a young freelance reporter working for the same paper. But Milne had lost his union card as a result of his refusal to support a strike in a provincial newspaper. Because a semi-official closed shop operated, a crisis had ensued and he had chosen to resign. Thus, though obliged to work with him because of his superior contacts, Wagner telexes a union official to ensure that his copy is not published. When, following Milne's death, Wagner himself gets a scoop, he is unable to use it as a result of the consequent union action which has closed his paper down.

His casual indifference to the wider implications of his own actions extends to his private life. The play takes place in the home of Geoffrey Carson, a mining engineer, whose wife, Ruth, had slept with Wagner on a brief visit to London. For Wagner, the world is one huge adventure playground, a separate moral universe, with its own childlike rules. Cause and effect are suspended. Actions are presumed to have no consequences. Hence he is equally blind to the fragile state of Ruth's mind and to the implications of his own parroting of radical slogans.

But Stoppard is careful to show that much the same could be said of Milne. As Ruth observes to Wagner, 'You're just like Jake, really . . . like Batman and Robin.' If Wagner reduces moral abstracts to political polemic, Milne raises the investigative potential of the press to the level of ethical absolute. And in the process he is as blind to human needs as is Wagner. He, too, is attracted to Ruth but fails equally to recognise her evident need for human contact. Wagner is trapped inside his own myth: that of the case-hardened professional and exploited worker. But Milne is equally caught up in his own. He is a white knight whose lack of professionalism endangers his own life and that of others. Both believe in the press, the one because it represents excitement, a world to conquer, a victory to be won over the vicissitudes of life, whether these take the form of getting the story back to London or fighting the established power of money and influence; the other because it is a necessary part of democratic freedoms. Both are equally contemptuous of the trivialisation of journalism; Wagner because it is unprofessional and hence demeans his self-image, Milne because it is tragically irrelevant and hence immoral.

Yet, in the context of the events outlined in the play, they are both equally manipulated, used by the very political forces which they observe. They are not simply employed as a conduit for information, as 'pigeons' to get propaganda out; they become part of the history which they imagine themselves simply to be reporting. Their hands are never entirely clean, though they see themselves as servants, and, on occasion, martyrs, to truth, or, as Wagner would say, facts. Both the rebel leader and the black dictator use the press as they do their armies, relying on a mutual self-interest which characterises Milne just as much as it does Wagner. And this is an irony which Stoppard, no less than Milne, leaves largely unexamined.

The difficulty of arguing for the central significance of a free press in a democracy, as Milne accepts, is that that freedom usually expresses itself in a farrago of trivia which debases reality rather than providing the necessary flow of information on which intelligent decisions may be made. Thus he is forced into the position of presenting those very trivia as evidence of a freedom which is squandered even as it is asserted. The value of a free press, he suggests, is not that it is invulnerable to influence, that it is accurate in its facts or even honourable in its intentions, but that it provides the constant possibility of exposure. There is something a little ponderous about these arguments, however, and the play's final irony is too carefully calculated for my taste. Milne dies trying to make a deadline, reporting a war which is conducted with total cynicism on both sides. Even the fact of his death will not be published because of the strike. He is killed by a reality which refuses to approximate itself to anybody else's principles. The most that can be said is that 'People do awful things to each other. But it's worse in places where everybody is kept in the dark. It really is. Information is light. Information, in itself, about anything, is light. That's all you can say, really.' The issues are deliberately not as clear as night and day, but this final comment by Guthrie, measured, limited, and yet authoritative, is clearly Stoppard's own and provides the real gloss on the play's title.

All of the play's characters are very much separate people. Ruth inhabits a solitary world, her husband is too busy with his business concerns and the affairs of state to recognise her human needs, and all three journalists are birds of passage, observers rather than fire fighters, operating according to a pragmatic ethic, while dignifying their actions with rhetoric or by reference to abstract values. Even Guthrie, in many ways a sympathetic character, suffers from a moral myopia which manifests itself in racial condescension and a failure to accord value to anything outside the immediate world of his professional competence. Hence, he places the total death toll in Viet Nam at fifty-four, this being the number of journalists to die. He remains unaware of the political situation which he is present to record. The world which he inhabits is not the complex one of colliding ideologies, of pressing moral dilemmas; it is a simple one whose limits are marked by immediate practical problems and whose values are little more than the code of a coterie of men who are dedicated to the belief that the appearance and essence of things coincides, that facts are synonymous with truth, and that the photograph constitutes an adequate account of the real. The events of the play show otherwise.

The journalists live by their own principles, which can apparently accommodate the need to lie, as Wagner does to Carson, to turn personal disaster into good copy, and to deprive an individual of his livelihood in an attempt to sustain a solidarity which is commercial rather than human. In that, of course, they are hardly inferior to the public and private worlds with which their own is coterminous. The irony is simply that they perform a potentially vital function for a society towards which they feel little responsibility and which they are potentially transforming from a complex reality into a series of simple formulae.

Ruth similarly remakes the world which she inhabits. The difficulty is that, with her, irony is pressing towards pathology. And this is a regression which can be dramatically confusing. For where at the beginning of the play her asides constitute a witty, if desperate, commentary on reality, by the beginning of the second act she has begun to substitute fantasy for that reality. Indeed, for a brief scene the dramatist only permits the audience to see the world through her eyes. Ruth and Milne apparently engage in a flirtatious and witty conversation, he, for the most part, resisting her advances, being anxious to contact London with his story and thus avoid the minor moral problems pursuant on sleeping with his host's wife. But it transpires that the whole scene has been enacted inside Ruth's head, that it is a fantasy projection of her emotional deprivation. Previously able to keep such fantasies at arm's length, she now substitutes illusion for reality. She lives, for a few minutes, in a world which she has Milne describe as 'a parallel world. No day or night, no responsibilities, no friction, almost no gravity.' And although, in a sense, this applies equally to the journalists, the analogy is not complete and, if theatrically effective, the interlude is a piece of adroit sleight of hand by the dramatist which poses questions about the nature of reality and the morality of art which remain unexamined. It also has the effect of making Ruth's state of mind rather too much the subject rather than the strategy of the play.

The difficulty, in fact, is that, as ever in Stoppard's work, there are several things going on at once. Alongside the central plot is another, of which Ruth is the focus. Her ability to commit herself emotionally at a moment's notice clearly fascinates Stoppard, but her arbitrary affections have only the most tenuous connection with the quixotic nature of journalistic life or the moral absolutes resolutely propounded but pragmatically set aside by Wagner and Milne. Our access to her private voice also inevitably moves her to the centre of dramatic attention in a way which is not sufficiently explained or utilised. Granted that she has herself suffered at the hands of the press, having been pursued by reporters during her divorce. But her own fierce assaults on the press seem unrelated to that experience and strangely at odds with a brittle emotional state which otherwise seeks release through a determined detachment from the real. Admittedly, she, like the journalists, is living a dramatised life, but her ironic self-mockery seems to stem from an emotional deprivation which has little connection with the events in which she plays such a deceptively significant part. She and Wagner end equally betrayed by events but the nature of that betrayal is sufficiently different in substance to prevent the two strands of the play from coming together with complete conviction.

Criticised for early work whose brilliance lacked moral substance, more recently Stoppard has combined his fascination with language and the nature of theatricality with a liberal resistance to a modern spirit of bogus rationalism and private and public pragmatism. The arrest, in Czechoslovakia, of the playwright Vaclav Havel, the threat to personal freedom represented by the harassment of dissidents in the Soviet Union and the proposals for a closed shop in British journalism, merely focussed an alarm which is implicit in a play like *Jumpers* and which derives from a fear that the individual is under assault from within and without. The liberal impulse seems ever harder to sustain, and the will to do so is continuously eroded by a materialism which takes both political and commercial form. Thus, his most recent plays have sought to identify that failure of nerve, to isolate those principles which, once abandoned, can be restored only with an effort which is as much imaginative as it is social or political. The wit with which the debate is conducted, however, is part of the guarantee that these values still exist, that there is still a space between appearance and reality, and that there remains room for the individual conscience to operate.

TOM STOPPARD
A Select Bibliography
(Place of publication London, unless otherwise stated)

Separate Works:

INTRODUCTIONS: Stories by New Writers (1964). *Fiction*
—includes 'Reunion', 'Life, Times, Fragments' and 'The Story' by Tom Stoppard.
LORD MALQUIST AND MR MOON (1966). *Fiction*
ROSENCRANTZ AND GUILDENSTERN ARE DEAD (1967). *Play*
ENTER A FREE MAN (1968). *Play*
THE REAL INSPECTOR HOUND (1968). *Play*
TANGO, by Sławomir Mrożek (1968). *Play*
—adapted by Tom Stoppard from the translation [from the Polish] by Nicholas Bethell.
ALBERT'S BRIDGE; AND, IF YOU'RE GLAD I'LL BE FRANK: Two plays for radio (1969).
A SEPARATE PEACE (1969). *Play*
AFTER MAGRITTE (1971). *Play*
JUMPERS (1972). *Play*
ARTIST DESCENDING A STAIRCASE; AND, WHERE ARE THEY NOW?: Two plays for radio (1973).
TRAVESTIES (1975). *Play*
DIRTY LINEN; AND, NEW-FOUND LAND (1976). *Plays*
EVERY GOOD BOY DESERVES FAVOUR; AND, PROFESSIONAL FOUL (1977). *Plays*
NIGHT AND DAY (1978). *Play*

Articles by Tom Stoppard:

'The Writer and the Theatre: The Definite Maybe', *Author*, 78, Spring 1967, 18–20.
'Something to Declare', *Sunday Times*, 25 February 1968.
'Doers and Thinkers; Playwrights and Professors', *Times Literary Supplement*, 13 October 1972, 1219.

Some Critical Studies:

ANGER AND AFTER, by J. Russell Taylor (1962)
—revised ed., 1969, includes a chapter on Tom Stoppard.
[Article] by John Simon, *Hudson Review*, 20, 4, Winter 1967–8, 664–5.
'The Devious Route to Waterloo Road', by Keith Harper, *Guardian*, 12 April 1967.
'Mini-Hamlets in limbo', by John Weightman, *Encounter*, 29, July 1967, 38–40.

'A Grin without a Cat', by Irving Wardle, *The Times*, 22 June 1968 —on *The Real Inspector Hound*.

'Absurdism altered: *Rosencrantz and Guildenstern are Dead*', by C. J. Gianakaris, *Drama Survey*, VII, Winter 1968, 52–8.

'Old and New in London Now', by Andrew K. Kennedy, *Modern Drama*, XI, February 1969, 437–46.

THE THIRD THEATRE, by Robert Brustein (1969) —'Waiting for Hamlet'.

'Stoppard's Godot: Some French influences on post-war English Drama', by Anthony Callen, *New Theatre Magazine*, 10, 1, Winter 1969, 22–30.

'The New Arrivals': No. 4. Tom Stoppard: Structure + Intellect', by J. Russell Taylor, *Plays and Players*, XVII, 10, July 1970, 16–18, 78.

'Rosencrantz and Guildenstern are alive and well in the classroom', by James E. Quinn, *Missouri English Bulletin*, 26 October 1970, 16–19.

'*Rosencrantz and Guildenstern are Dead*', by Walter D. Asmus, *Jahrbuch der Deutschen Shakespeare-Gesellschaft West*, 1970, 118–31.

THE SECOND WAVE: British Drama for the Seventies, by J. Russell Taylor (1971).

'They have their Entrances and their Exits: *Rosencrantz and Guildenstern are Dead*', by Peter Carroll, *Teaching of English*, 20, 1971, 50–60.

'Views from a Revolving Door: Tom Stoppard's Career to date', by Jill Levenson, *Queen's Quarterly*, 58, 1971, 431–42.

'Love among the Logical Positivists: *Jumpers*', by A. J. Ayer, *Sunday Times*, 9 April 1972, 16.

'A Metaphysical Comedy', by John Weightman, *Encounter*, 38, April 1972, 44–6.

'At Lady Muldoon's', by Edith Oliver, *New Yorker*, 6 May 1972, 61–2.

[Article] by J. W. Lambert, *Drama*, Summer 1972, 15.

'The Play-Life Metaphor in Shakespeare and Stoppard', by William Babula, *Modern Drama*, XV, December 1972, 279–81.

'*Rosencrantz and Guildenstern are Dead*: Theater of Criticism', by Normand Berlin, *Modern Drama*, XVI, December 1973, 269–77.

[Article] by Adrian Rendle, *Drama*, Winter 1973, 88.

'The Joke's the Thing', by Mark Amory, *Sunday Times Magazine*, 9 June 1974, 64.

'The Zealots of Zurich', Richard Ellmann, *Times Literary Supplement*, 12 July 1974, 744.

'Philosophy and Mr Stoppard', by Jonathan Bennett, *Philosophy*, 50, January 1975, 5–18.

CONTEMPORARY LITERARY CRITICISM: Excerpts from Criticism of the Works of Today's Novelists, Poets, Playwrights, and other creative writers, ed. Carolyn Riley; Detroit (1975)

—Vols III and IV contain extracts from criticism and reviews of Stoppard's *Rosencrantz and Guildenstern are Dead* and *Jumpers*.

'The Circle and its Tangent', by R. H. Lee, *Theoria*, XXXIII, 37-43
—a study of *Rosencrantz and Guildenstern are Dead*.

'The Circle and its Tangent', by R. H. Lee, *Theoria*, XXXIII, 37-43
—a study *of Rosencrantz and Guildenstern are Dead*.

TOM STOPPARD, by Ronald Hayman (1977)

Interviews:

BEHIND THE SCENES: Theatre and film interviews from the *Transatlantic Review*, ed. J. F. McCrindle (1971)
—records an interview with Giles Gordon in 1968.

[Interview with Janet Watts], *Guardian*, 21 March 1973.

'The Translators: Tom Stoppard', *Plays and Players*, 20, 7, April 1973, 36-7
—interview with Michael Leech discussing Garcia Lorca's *The House of Bernarda Alba*.

'Ambushes for the Audience: Towards a High Comedy of Ideas', *Theatre Quarterly*, May-July 1974, 3-17
—with Roger Hudson, Catherine Itzin and Simon Trussler.

'Writing's my 43rd priority', *Observer*, 17 December 1967
—interview with John Gale.

WRITERS AND THEIR WORK

General Surveys:
THE DETECTIVE STORY IN BRITAIN: Julian Symons
THE ENGLISH BIBLE: Donald Coggan
ENGLISH VERSE EPIGRAM: G. Rostrevor Hamilton
ENGLISH HYMNS: Arthur Pollard
ENGLISH MARITIME WRITING: Hakluyt to Cook: Oliver Warner
THE ENGLISH SHORT STORY I: & II: T. O. Beachcroft
THE ENGLISH SONNET: P. Cruttwell
ENGLISH SERMONS: Arthur Pollard
ENGLISH TRANSLATORS AND TRANSLATIONS: J. M. Cohen
ENGLISH TRAVELLERS IN THE NEAR EAST: Robin Fedden
THREE WOMEN DIARISTS: M. Willy

Sixteenth Century and Earlier:
FRANCIS BACON: J. Max Patrick
BEAUMONT & FLETCHER: Ian Fletcher
CHAUCER: Nevill Coghill
GOWER & LYDGATE: Derek Pearsall
RICHARD HOOKER: Arthur Pollard
THOMAS KYD: Philip Edwards
LANGLAND: Nevill Coghill
LYLY & PEELE: G. K. Hunter
MALORY: M. C. Bradbrook
MARLOWE: Philip Henderson
SIR THOMAS MORE: E. E. Reynolds
RALEGH: Agnes Latham
SIDNEY: Kenneth Muir
SKELTON: Peter Green
SPENSER: Rosemary Freeman
THREE 14TH-CENTURY ENGLISH MYSTICS: Phyllis Hodgson
TWO SCOTS CHAUCERIANS: H. Harvey Wood
WYATT: Sergio Baldi

Seventeenth Century:
SIR THOMAS BROWNE: Peter Green
BUNYAN: Henri Talon
CAVALIER POETS: Robin Skelton
CONGREVE: Bonamy Dobrée
DONNE: F. Kermode
DRYDEN: Bonamy Dobrée
ENGLISH DIARISTS: Evelyn and Pepys: M. Willy
FARQUHAR: A. J. Farmer
JOHN FORD: Clifford Leech
GEORGE HERBERT: T. S. Eliot
HERRICK: John Press
HOBBES: T. E. Jessop
BEN JONSON: J. B. Bamborough
LOCKE: Maurice Cranston
ANDREW MARVELL: John Press
MILTON: E. M. W. Tillyard
RESTORATION COURT POETS: V. de S. Pinto
SHAKESPEARE: C. J. Sisson
　CHRONICLES: Clifford Leech
　EARLY COMEDIES: Derek Traversi
　LATER COMEDIES: G. K. Hunter
　FINAL PLAYS: F. Kermode
　HISTORIES: L. C. Knights
　POEMS: F. T. Prince
　PROBLEM PLAYS: Peter Ure
　ROMAN PLAYS: T. J. B. Spencer
　GREAT TRAGEDIES: Kenneth Muir
THREE METAPHYSICAL POETS: Margaret Willy
WEBSTER: Ian Scott-Kilvert
WYCHERLEY: P. F. Vernon

Eighteenth Century:
BERKELEY: T. E. Jessop
BLAKE: Kathleen Raine
BOSWELL: P. A. W. Collins
BURKE: T. E. Utley
BURNS: David Daiches
WM COLLINS: Oswald Doughty
COWPER: N. Nicholson
CRABBE: R. L. Brett
DEFOE: J. R. Sutherland
FIELDING: John Butt
GAY: Oliver Warner
GIBBON: C. V. Wedgwood
GOLDSMITH: A. Norman Jeffares
GRAY: R. W. Ketton-Cremer

HUME: Montgomery Belgion
SAMUEL JOHNSON: S. C. Roberts
POPE: Ian Jack
RICHARDSON: R. F. Brissenden
SHERIDAN: W. A. Darlington
CHRISTOPHER SMART: G. Grigson
SMOLLETT: Laurence Brander
STEELE, ADDISON: A. R. Humphreys
STERNE: D. W. Jefferson
SWIFT: J. Middleton Murry
SIR JOHN VANBRUGH: Bernard Harris
HORACE WALPOLE: Hugh Honour

Nineteenth Century:
MATTHEW ARNOLD: Kenneth Allott
JANE AUSTEN: S. Townsend Warner
BAGEHOT: N. St John-Stevas
THE BRONTËS: I & II: Winifred Gérin
BROWNING: John Bryson
E. B. BROWNING: Alethea Hayter
SAMUEL BUTLER: G. D. H. Cole
BYRON: I, II & III:
                Bernard Blackstone
CARLYLE: David Gascoyne
LEWIS CARROLL: Derek Hudson
COLERIDGE: Kathleen Raine
CREEVEY & GREVILLE: J. Richardson
DE QUINCEY: Hugh Sykes Davies
DICKENS: K. J. Fielding
   EARLY NOVELS: T. Blount
   LATER NOVELS: B. Hardy
DISRAELI: Paul Bloomfield
GEORGE ELIOT: Lettice Cooper
FERRIER & GALT: W. M. Parker
FITZGERALD: Joanna Richardson
ELIZABETH GASKELL: Miriam Allott
GISSING: A. C. Ward
THOMAS HARDY: R. A. Scott-James
                and C. Day Lewis
HAZLITT: J. B. Priestley
HOOD: Laurence Brander
G. M. HOPKINS: Geoffrey Grigson
T. H. HUXLEY: William Irvine
KEATS: Edmund Blunden
LAMB: Edmund Blunden
LANDOR: G. Rostrevor Hamilton
EDWARD LEAR: Joanna Richardson
MACAULAY: G. R. Potter

MEREDITH: Phyllis Bartlett
JOHN STUART MILL: M. Cranston
WILLIAM MORRIS: P. Henderson
NEWMAN: J. M. Cameron
PATER: Ian Fletcher
PEACOCK: J. I. M. Stewart
ROSSETTI: Oswald Doughty
CHRISTINA ROSSETTI: G. Battiscombe
RUSKIN: Peter Quennell
SIR WALTER SCOTT: Ian Jack
SHELLEY: G. M. Matthews
SOUTHEY: Geoffrey Carnall
LESLIE STEPHEN: Phyllis Grosskurth
R. L. STEVENSON: G. B. Stern
SWINBURNE: Ian Fletcher
TENNYSON: B. C. Southam
THACKERAY: Laurence Brander
FRANCIS THOMPSON: P. Butter
TROLLOPE: Hugh Sykes Davies
OSCAR WILDE: James Laver
WORDSWORTH: Helen Darbishire

Twentieth Century:
CHINUA ACHEBE: A. Ravenscroft
JOHN ARDEN: Glenda Leeming
W. H. AUDEN: Richard Hoggart
SAMUEL BECKETT: J-J. Mayoux
HILAIRE BELLOC: Renée Haynes
ARNOLD BENNETT: Kenneth Young
JOHN BETJEMAN: John Press
EDMUND BLUNDEN: Alec M. Hardie
ROBERT BRIDGES: J. Sparrow
ANTHONY BURGESS: Carol M. Dix
ROY CAMPBELL: David Wright
JOYCE CARY: Walter Allen
G. K. CHESTERTON: C. Hollis
WINSTON CHURCHILL: John Connell
R. G. COLLINGWOOD: E. W. F. Tomlin
I. COMPTON-BURNETT:
                R. Glynn Grylls
JOSEPH CONRAD: Oliver Warner
WALTER DE LA MARE: K. Hopkins
NORMAN DOUGLAS: Ian Greenlees
LAWRENCE DURRELL: G. S. Fraser
T. S. ELIOT: M. C. Bradbrook
T. S. ELIOT: The Making of
  'The Waste Land': M. C. Bradbrook